HAL•LEONARD®

DRUM PLAY-ALONG™

AUDIO
ACCESS
INCLUDED

MÖTLEY CRÜE

PLAYBACK+
Speed • Pitch • Balance • Loop

To access audio visit:
www.halleonard.com/mylibrary

Enter Code
2033-6377-6660-2564

Cover Photo: Paul Brown

ISBN 978-1-4950-7919-1

HAL•LEONARD®
7777 W. BLUEMOUND RD. P.O. BOX 13819 MILWAUKEE, WI 53213

In Australia Contact:
Hal Leonard Australia Pty. Ltd.
4 Lentara Court
Cheltenham, Victoria, 3192 Australia
Email: ausadmin@halleonard.com.au

CONTENTS

Dr. Feelgood

Words by Nikki Sixx
Music by Nikki Sixx and Mick Mars

Intro
Moderate Rock ♩ = 111

𝄋 **Verse**

1. Rat - tailed Jim - my is a sec - ond - hand hood, deals

2., 3. See additional lyrics

___ out in Hol - ly - wood. ___ Got a six - ty - five Chev - y, prim - ered flames, ___

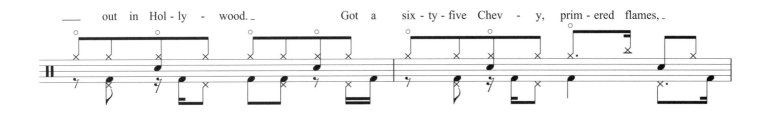

trad - ed for some pow - dered goods. ___ Jig - saw Jim - my, he's a, run - nin' a gang, ___ but I

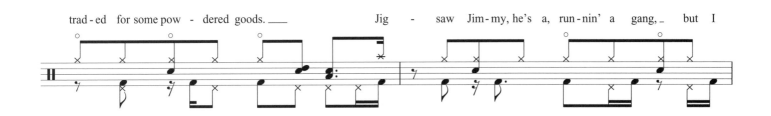

To Coda ⊕

hear he's do - in' o - kay. Got a co - zy lit - tle job, sells the Mex - i - can mob

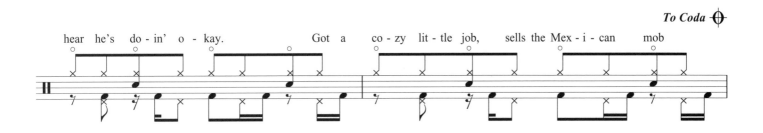

Chorus

pack - ag - es of can - dy - caine. ___ He's ___ the one they call Doc - tor Feel - good. ___ He's ___

___ the one that makes you feel al - right. He's ___ the one they call Doc - tor Feel - good. ___

5

Bridge

Guitar Solo

D.S. al Coda

3. He'll

⊕ Coda

Chorus

Interlude

Bridge

Huh! I've _____ got one thing you'll un - der - stand. ___

_____ He's not ___ what you'd call a glam - 'rous man. _____ Got ___

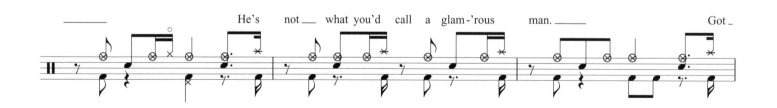

___ one thing that's eas - i - ly un - der - stood. _____ He's _

8

the one they call Doc - tor Feel - good. _____ Whoa! _

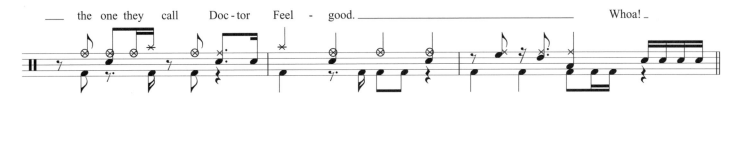

Outro

Fade out

Additional Lyrics

2. Cops on the corner always ignore. Somebody's gettin' paid.
   Jimmy's got it wired; law's for hire. Got it made in the shade.
   Got a little hideaway, does bus'ness all day, but at night he'll always be found
   Sellin' sugar to the sweet people on the street. Call this Jimmy's town.

3. He'll tell you he's the king of these barrio streets, movin' up to Shangri-La.
   Came by his wealth as a matter of luck, says he never broke no law.
   Two-time loser, runnin' outta juice, time to move out quick.
   Heard a rumor goin' 'round, Jimmy's goin' down. This time it's gonna stick.

Kickstart My Heart

Words and Music by Nikki Sixx

drug   for   me. ___   My   heart, ___   my   heart, ___   kick - start   my   heart. ___

_____

Al - ways got the cops   com - in'

af - ter   me, _____   cus - tom - built   bike   do - in'   one - oh - three.   My   heart, __

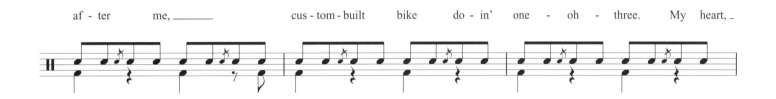

___   my   heart, __   kick - start   my   heart. ____

Pre-Chorus
Oo,   are   you   read - y,   girls? _____   Oo,   are   you

𝄉 **Chorus**
read - y   now? _   Whoa, _____   yeah, _____   kick -

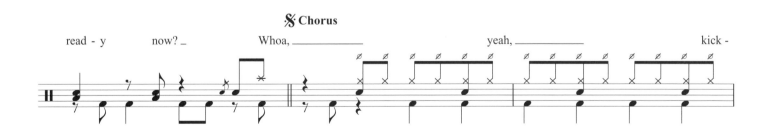

- start my heart,   give   it   a   start. _   Whoa, _____   yeah, _

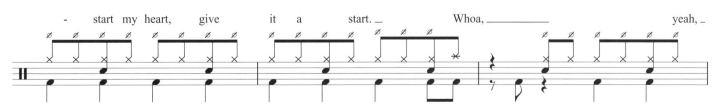

ba - by. _____ Whoa, _

To Coda ⊕

yeah, _____ kick - start my heart, hope it

nev - er stops. _ Whoa, _____ yeah, _____

ba - by, _____ yeah. _____

Interlude

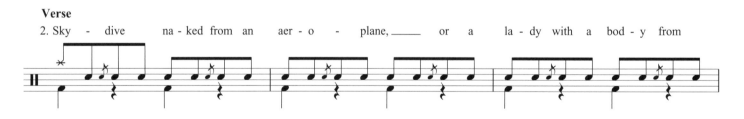

Verse

2. Sky - dive na - ked from an aer - o - plane, _____ or a la - dy with a bod - y from

Fill 1

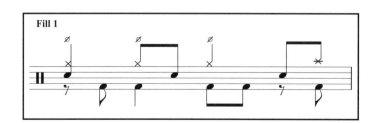

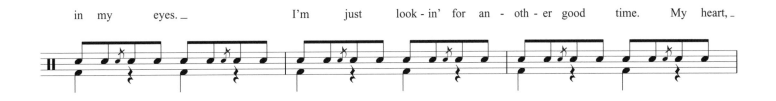

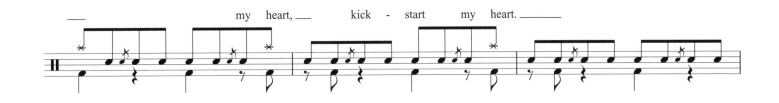

Pre-Chorus

Chorus

Interlude

Bridge

Guitar Solo

ba - by. _____

Chorus

Whoa, _____ yeah, _____

_____ kick - start my heart, hope it nev - er stops. _____ Whoa, _____

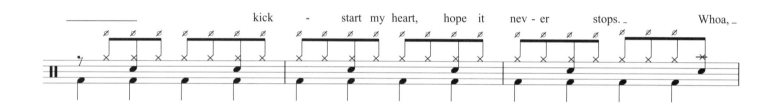

_____ yeah, _____ ba - by. _____

_____ Whoa, _____ yeah, _____ kick -

- start my heart, give it a start. _____ Whoa, _____ yeah. _____

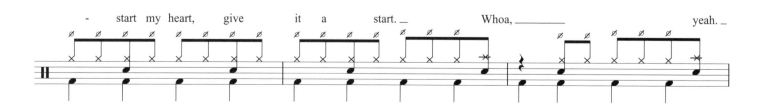

O.　K.　boys, ＿　let's　rock　the　house! ＿＿＿＿＿＿＿

Outro

Free time

Girls, Girls, Girls

Words by Nikki Sixx
Music by Nikki Sixx, Tommy Lee and Mick Mars

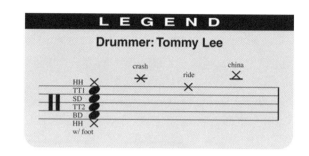

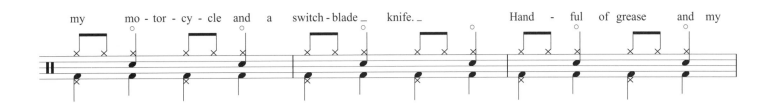

my mo - tor - cy - cle and a switch - blade __ knife. __ Hand - ful of grease and my

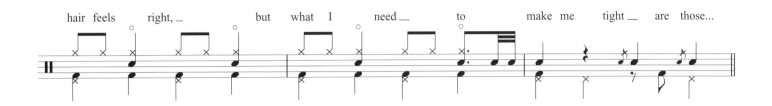

hair feels right, __ but what I need __ to make me tight __ are those...

Chorus

Girls, girls, girls. __ Long legs and bur - gun - dy lips. __

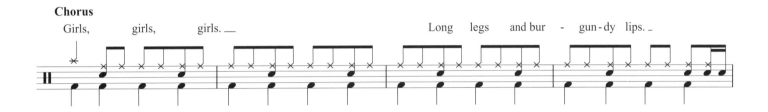

Girls, girls, girls. __ Danc - in' down __ on the Sun - set __ Strip. __

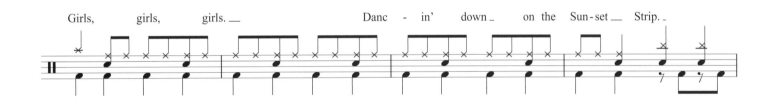

Girls, girls, girls. ___ Red lips,

Verse

fin - ger - tips. __ 2. Trick or treat, sweet to eat ___

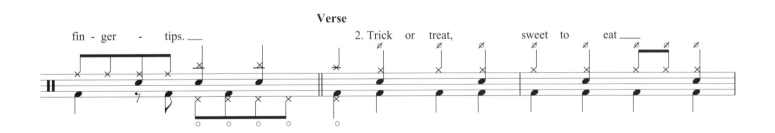

on Hal - low - een and New Year's Eve. __ Yan - kee girls, __ ya just

can't be beat, ___ but you're the best ___ when you're off ___ your feet. ___

Chorus

Girls, girls, girls. ___ At the Doll - house in Fort Lau - der - dale.

Girls, girls, girls. ___ Rock - in' in At - lan - ta at Tat - tle - tails. ___

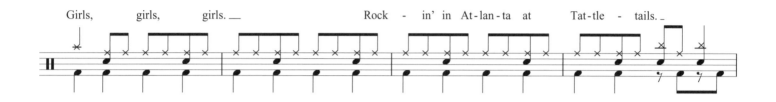

Girls, girls, girls. ___ Rais - in' hell at the

Bridge

Sev - enth Veil. ___ Have you read the news ___ in the

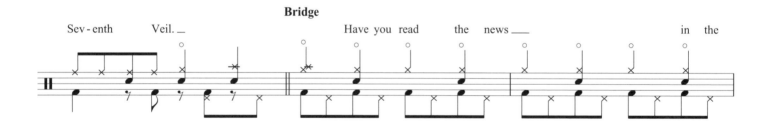

So - Ho Trib - une? ___ Ya know she did ___ me, ___

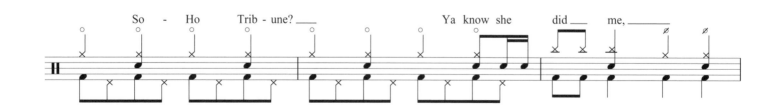

well, then she broke ___ my heart. ___ I'm such a good, good

Interlude

Verse

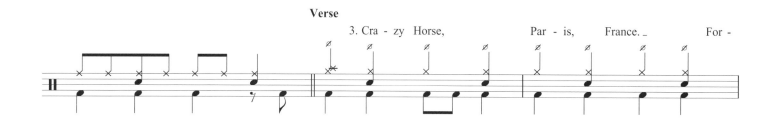

3. Cra - zy Horse, Par - is, France. For -

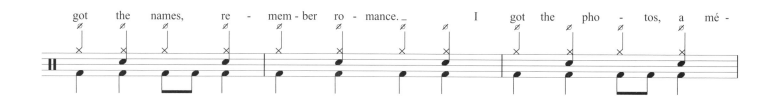

got the names, re - mem - ber ro - mance. I got the pho - tos, a mé -

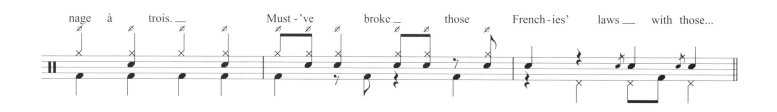

nage à trois. Must -'ve broke those French -ies' laws with those...

Chorus

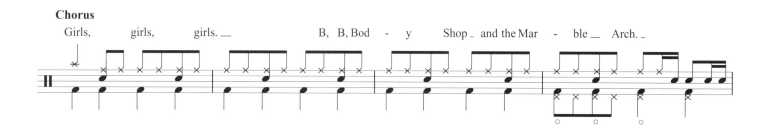

Girls, girls, girls. B, B, Bod - y Shop and the Mar - ble Arch.

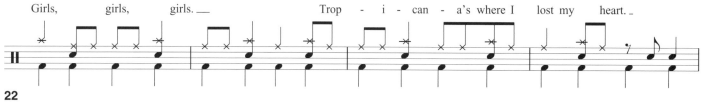

Girls, girls, girls. Trop - i - can - a's where I lost my heart.

Spoken: Hey Tommy,

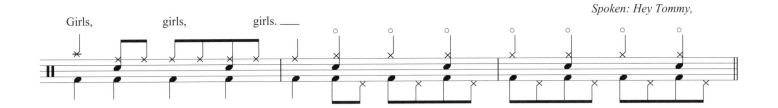

Girls,   girls,   girls. ___

Interlude

check that out, man.   *Hey, right there.*   *Hey baby, don't I know you from*

Spoken: What, Vince, where?   *Hey!*

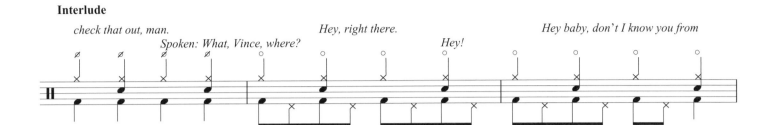

somewhere?

Girls,   girls,   girls. ___

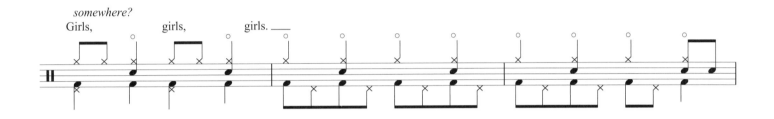

Girls,   girls,   girls. ___

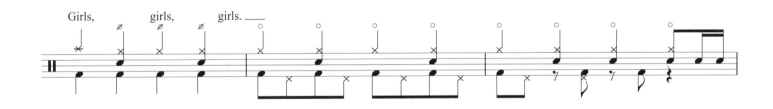

Girls,   girls,   girls. ___

Girls,   girls,   girls. ___

Outro-Guitar Solo

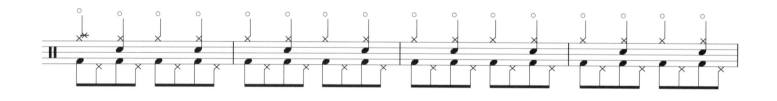

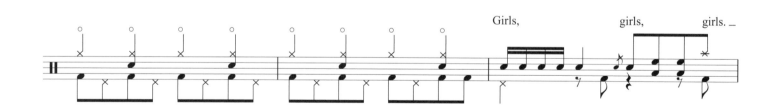

Girls,   girls,   girls.

Free time

Live Wire

Words and Music by Nikki Sixx

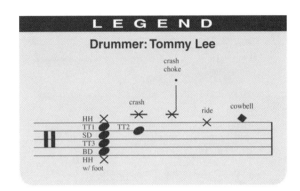

Intro
Moderately fast Rock ♩ = 112
Double-time feel

1. Plug

%. **Verse**

___ me in, I'm a-live to-night, ___ out on the streets ___ a-gain. ___ Turn ___
2. *See additional lyrics*

___ me on, I'm too hot to stop, ___ some-thing you'll nev - er for - get. ___ Take ___

___ my fist to break ___ down walls, ___ on top to - night. ___ No, ___

no.   Bet - ter turn me   loose. _   Bet - ter set me   free, _ 'cause I'm a,

To Coda

hot and a, young,   run - nin' free, _   lit - tle bit bet - ter than I used to be. _ 'Cause I'm a -

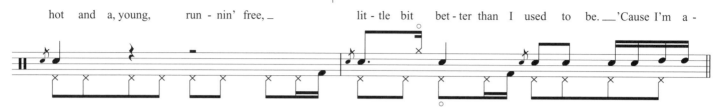

Chorus

live,   live wire. _____   'Cause I'm a - live,   I'm _ a live

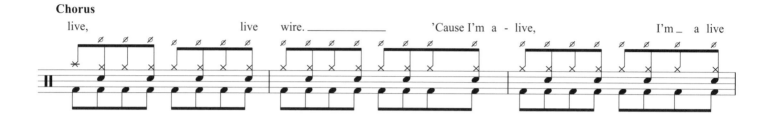

wire. _____ 'Cause I'm a - live,   live

wire. _____ 'Cause I'm a - live,   I'm _ a live wire. _____

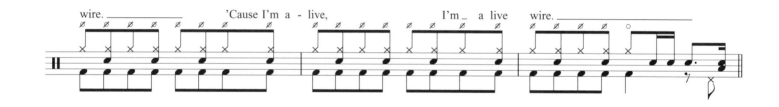

Interlude

2. I'll ei-ther

⊕ Coda

Chorus

lit - tle bit   bet - ter than I used   to be. __'Cause I'm a - live,   live

wire. _____   'Cause I'm   a - live,   I'm __ a live

wire. _____   'Cause I'm   a - live,   live

End double-time feel

wire. _____   'Cause I'm a - live,   I'm _ a live   wire. _____

Interlude
Slower ♩ = 103

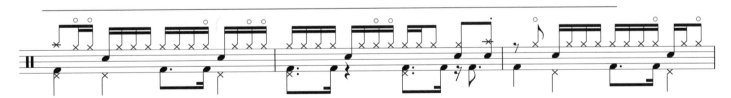

Ooh.   **Bridge**   Come on,   ba - by, __

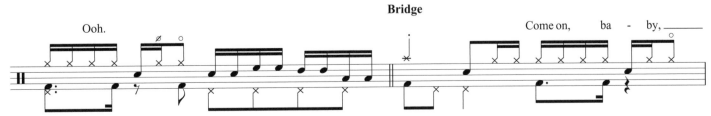

got-ta play with me. ___ Well, I'm your live wire, __ yeah. _____

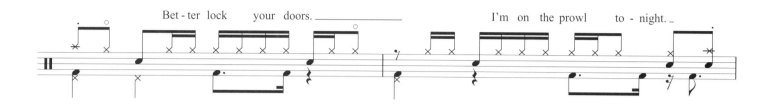

Bet - ter lock your doors. _____ I'm on the prowl to - night. _

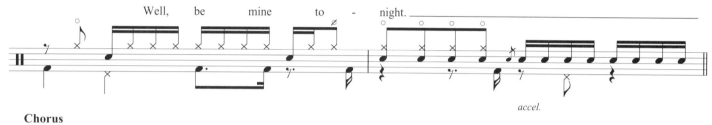

Well, be mine to - night. _____

accel.

Chorus
Tempo I
Double-time feel

_____ 'Cause I'm a - live, live

wire. _____ 'Cause I'm a - live, I'm_ a live

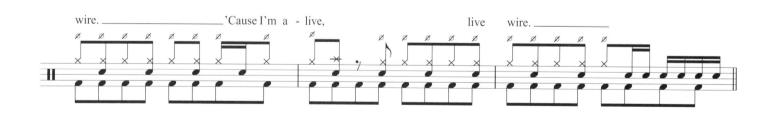

wire. _____'Cause I'm a - live, live wire. _____

Outro

Come on, be _ my ba - by. Come on to - night. _____

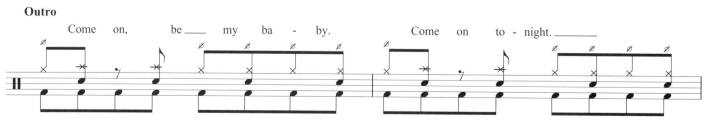

Additional Lyrics

2. I'll either break her face or take down her legs, gettin' my face at will.
   Go for the throat and never let loose, goin' in for the kill.
   Take my fist and break down walls, on top tonight. No, no.
   Better turn me loose. You better set me free,
   'Cause I'm a, hot, and a, young, runnin' free, a little bit better than I used to be.

Looks That Kill

Words and Music by Nikki Sixx

Yeah.

Interlude

Hey!

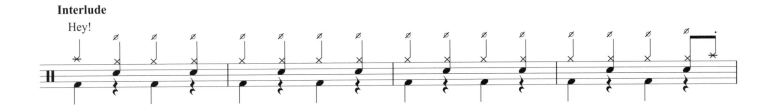

D.S. al Coda
(take 2nd ending)

3. Now lis -

(Hey!)

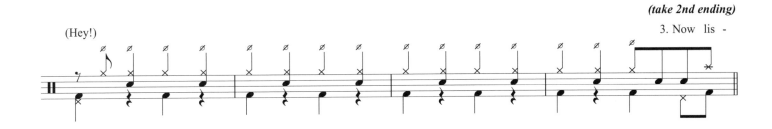

Coda

Interlude

looks that kill.) __

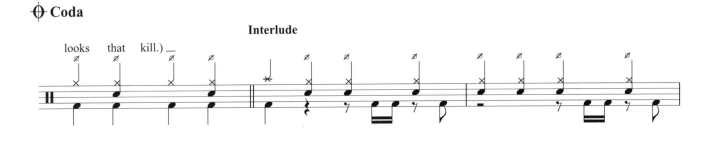

(She's got the looks that kill. __

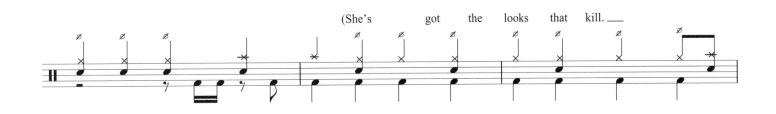

Outro

She's got the looks that kill.) __ (She's got the

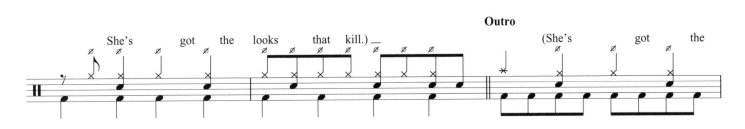

Begin fade

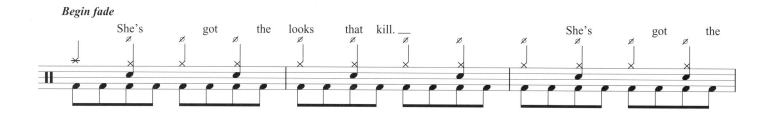

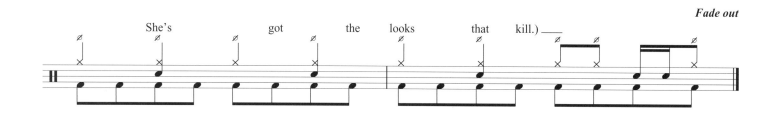

Fade out

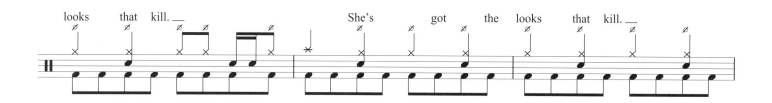

Additional Lyrics

2. Now she's bulletproof. She keeps her motor clean.
   Oo, and believe me, you, she's a number thirteen.
   The church strikes midnight. She's looking louder and louder.
   She's gonna turn on your juice, boy, oh, then she'll turn on the power.

3. Now listen up. She's a, razor sharp.
   If she don't get her way, she'll slice you apart.
   Well, she's a cool, cool black, moves like a cat.
   If you don't get her game, you might not make it back.

Shout at the Devil

Words and Music by Nikki Sixx

Intro
Moderate Rock ♩ = 95

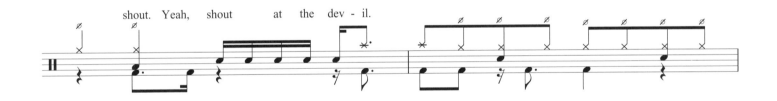

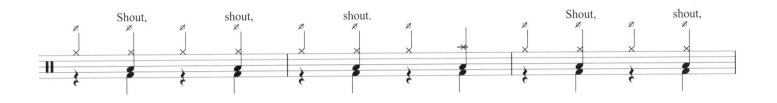

Verse

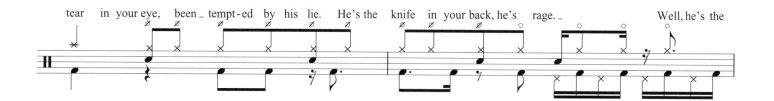

tear in your eye, been tempt-ed by his lie. He's the knife in your back, he's rage. Well, he's the

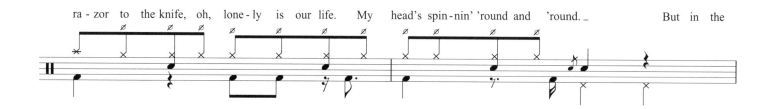

ra-zor to the knife, oh, lone-ly is our life. My head's spin-nin' 'round and 'round. But in the

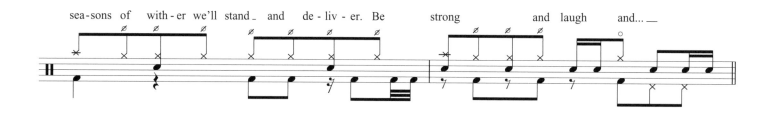

sea-sons of with-er we'll stand and de-liv-er. Be strong and laugh and...

Chorus

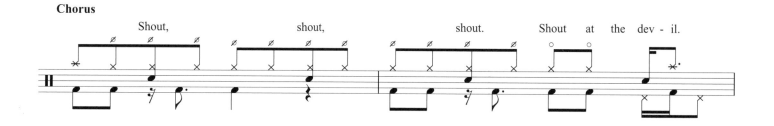

Shout, shout, shout. Shout at the dev-il.

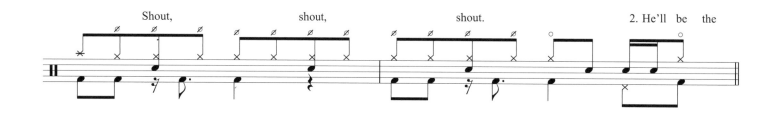

Shout, shout, shout. 2. He'll be the

Verse

love in your eyes, he'll be the blood be-tween your thighs, and then he'll have you cry for more. He'll put your

strength to the test, he'll put the thrill back in death. I'm sure you've heard it all be-fore. He'll be the risk in the kiss, might be an - ger on your lips, might run scared for the door. _____ But in the

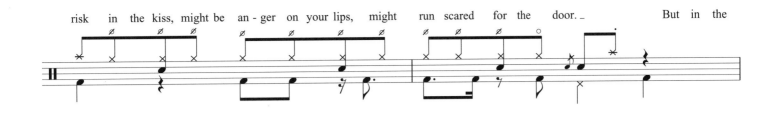

sea - sons of with - er, we'll stand _ and de - liv - er. Be strong and laugh and...

Chorus

Shout, shout, shout. Shout at the dev - il. Shout, shout,

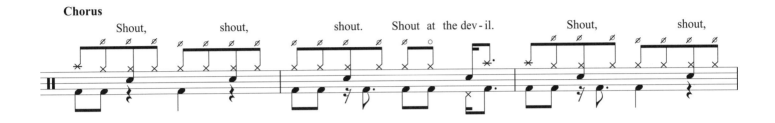

shout. Shout at the dev - il.

Guitar Solo

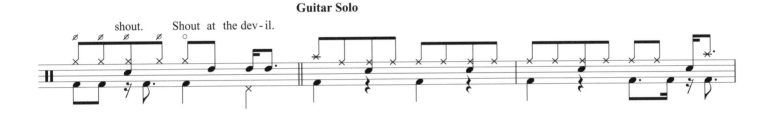

Verse

3. He's the wolf scream - ing lone - ly in the night. He's the blood - stain on the stage. _____ He's the

tear in your eye, been _ tempt - ed by his lie. He's the knife in your back, he's rage. _ Well, he's the

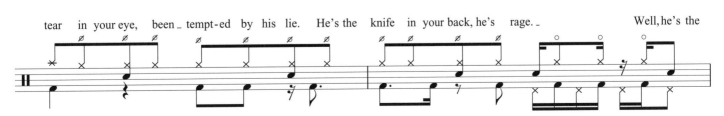

37

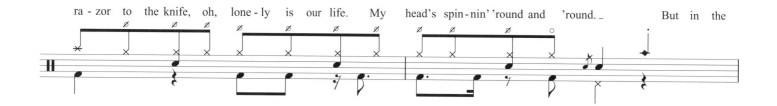

ra - zor to the knife, oh, lone - ly is our life. My head's spin-nin' 'round and 'round._ But in the

sea-sons of with-er we'll stand _ and de - liv - er. Be strong and laugh and... _

Chorus

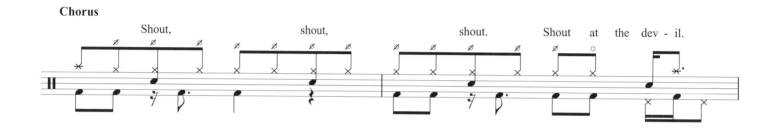

Shout, shout, shout. Shout at the dev - il.

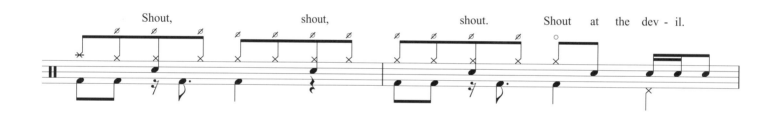

Shout, shout, shout. Shout at the dev - il.

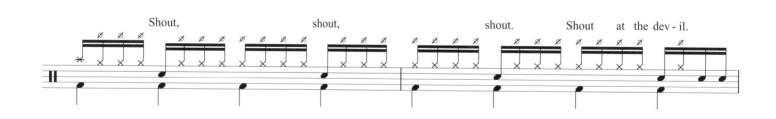

Shout, shout, shout. Shout at the dev - il.

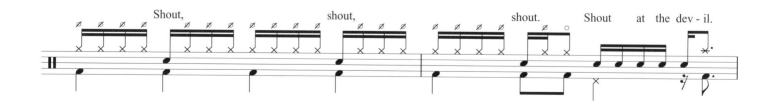

Shout, shout, shout. Shout at the dev - il.

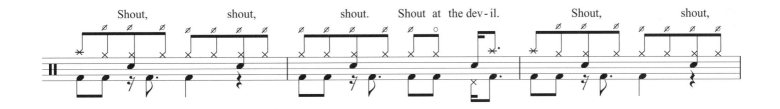

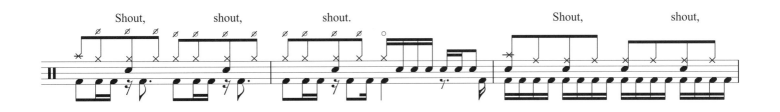

Too Young to Fall in Love

Words and Music by Nikki Sixx

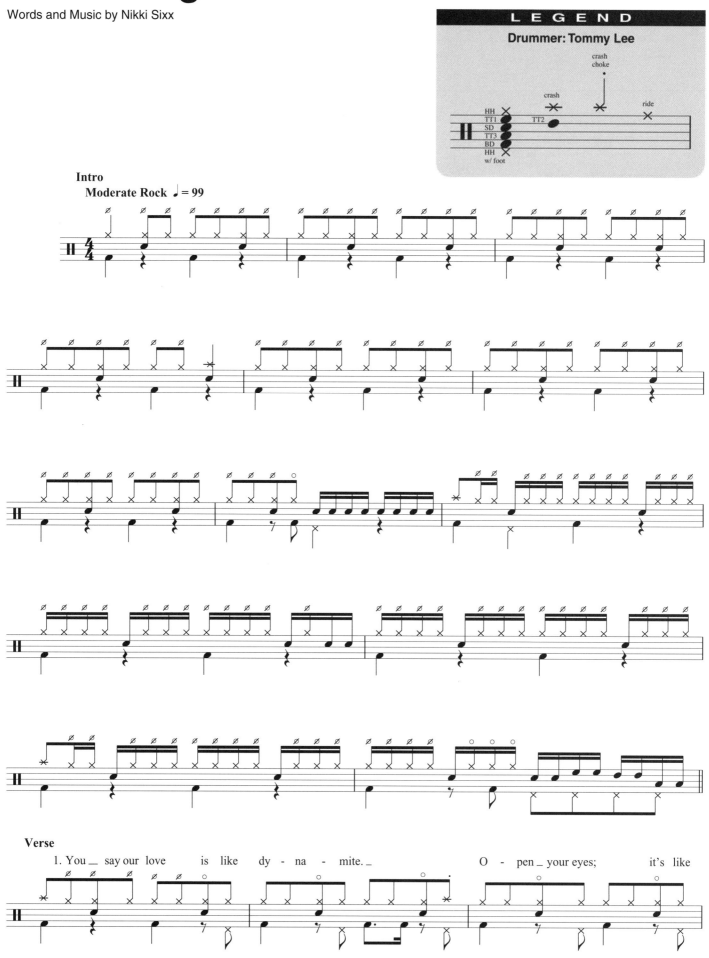

sin-ners and _ saints. _ Not a wom-an but a whore; I can taste the _ hate. _ Well,

now I'm kill-in' you, _ watch your face turn-in' blue. _

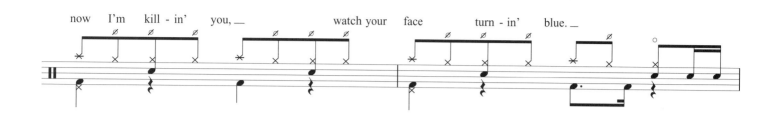

Not yet _ a man, _ just a punk in the street. _____ Yeah! _

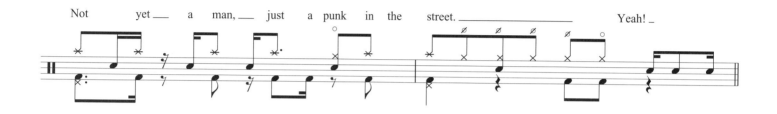

Chorus

(Too young to fall in love. _____ Too young to fall in love. _____

Too young to fall in love. _____

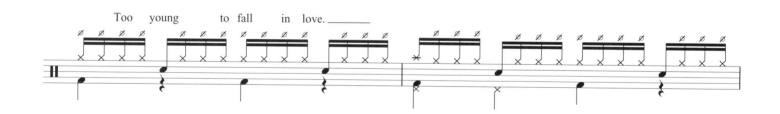

Too young to fall in love. _____ Too young to fall in love. _____

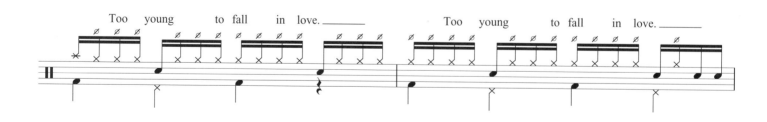

Guitar Solo

Too young to fall in love.) _____

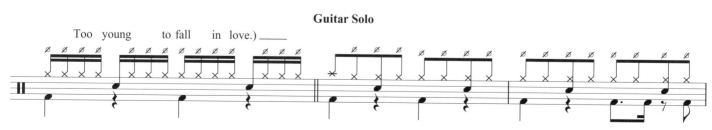

Interlude

Verse

3. You __ say our love is like dy - na - mite. __ It's no sur - prise __ 'cause you've got

one - way __ eyes. __ Well, you're kill-in' me. __ Your love's a guil-lo - tine.

Not yet __ a man, __ just a punk in the street. __ Yeah! __

Chorus

(Too young to fall in love. _____ Too young to fall in love. _____

Too young to fall in love. _____

Too young to fall in love. _____ Too young to fall in love. _____

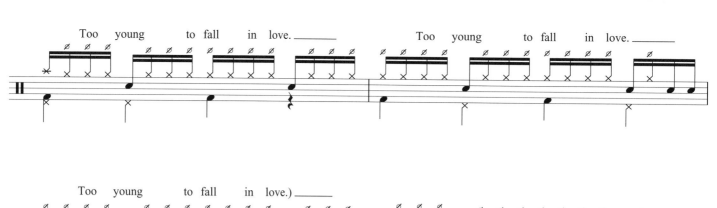

Too young to fall in love.) _____

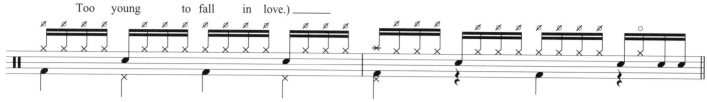

Outro

Too young to fall in love. _____ Too young to fall in love. _____ Too young to fall in love. _____

Begin fade

Too young to fall in love. _____ Too young to fall in love. _____

Too young to fall in love. _____

Too young to fall in love. _____ Too young to fall in love. _____ Too young to fall in love. _____

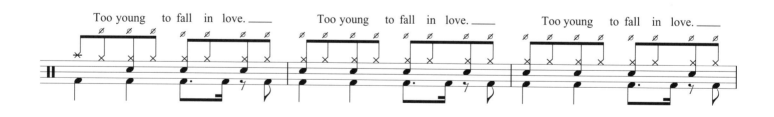

Fade out

Too young to fall in love. _____ Too young to fall in love.) _____

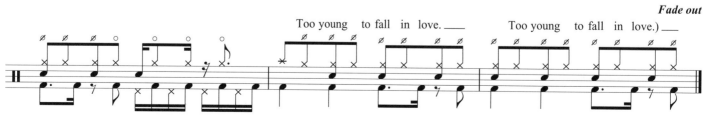

Wild Side

Words by Nikki Sixx
Music by Nikki Sixx, Tommy Lee and Vince Neil

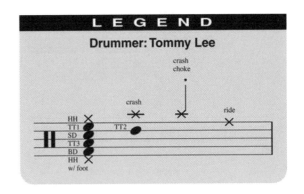

𝄋 Verse

2nd time, substitute Fill 1

1. Kneel down, you sin - ners, to street - wise re - li - gion. Greed's

2., 3. *See additional lyrics*

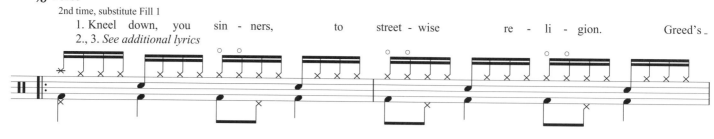

___ been crowned ___ the new king. _____

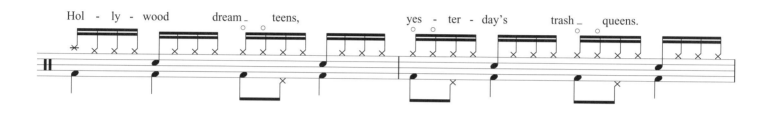

Hol - ly - wood dream ___ teens, yes - ter - day's trash ___ queens.

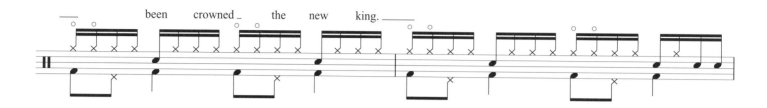

2nd time, substitute Fill 2
3rd time, substitute Fill 3

Save the bless - ings for the fi - nal _____ ring. ____ A - men!

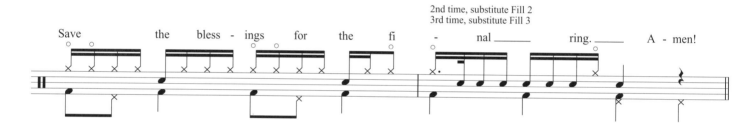

Chorus

Take a ride on the wi - ld ___ side. ___

Fill 1

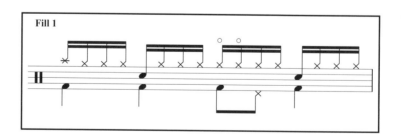

Fill 2

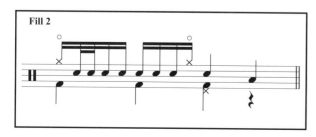

Fill 3

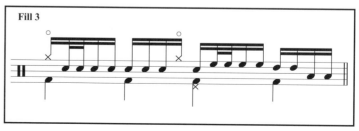

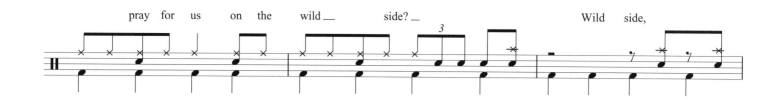

pray   for   us   on   the   wild __   side? __   Wild   side,

(♫ = ♫)

wild   side.

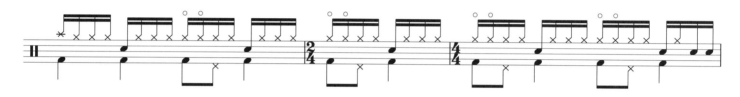

Interlude

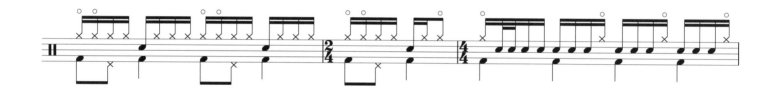

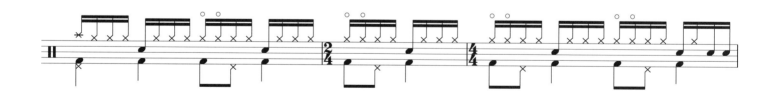

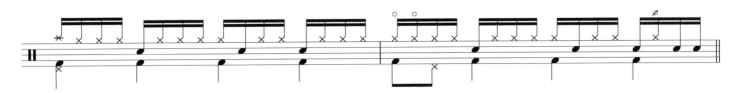

Coda

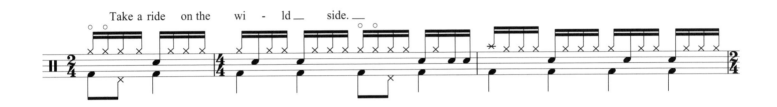

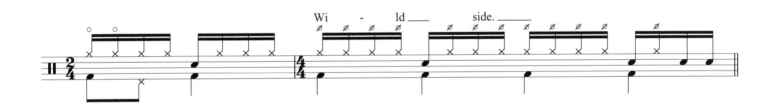

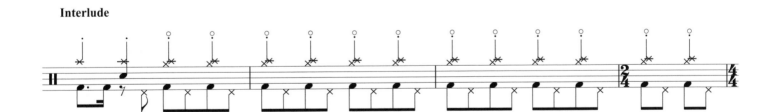

Interlude

Outro

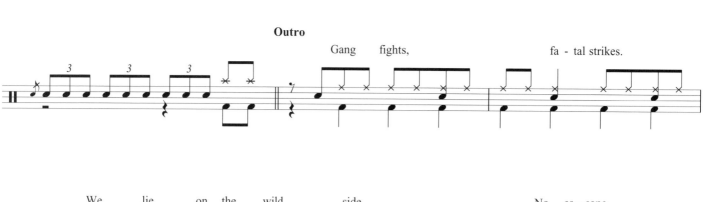

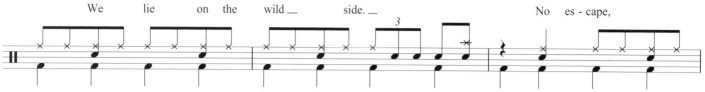

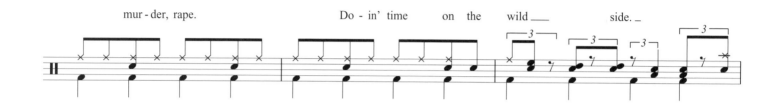

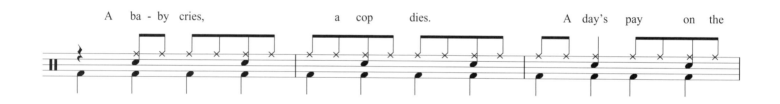

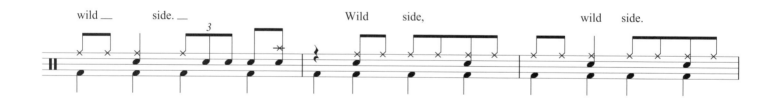

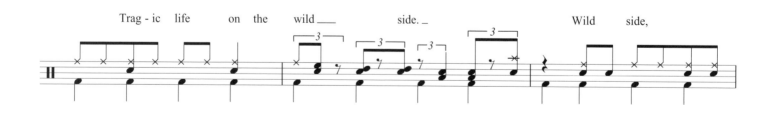

Now we're back   on   the

wild ___   side. ___

Begin fade

Fade out

Additional Lyrics

2. I carry my crucifix under my death list.
   Forward my mail to me in hell.
   Liars and the martyrs lost faith in the father.
   Long lost is the wishing well. Huh!

3. Name dropping no-names, glamorize cocaine.
   Puppets with strings of gold.
   East L.A. at midnight, Papa won't be home tonight.
   Found dead with his best friend's wife.

HAL•LEONARD DRUM PLAY-ALONG

Play your favorite songs quickly and easily with the *Drum Play-Along*™ series. Just follow the drum notation, listen to the CD or online audio to hear how the drums should sound, then play along using the separate backing tracks. The lyrics are also included for quick reference. The audio CD is playable on any CD player. For PC and Mac computer users, the CD is enhanced so you can adjust the recording to any tempo without changing the pitch!

Prices, contents and availability subject to change without notice and may vary outside the US.

HAL•LEONARD® CORPORATION
7777 W. BLUEMOUND RD. P.O. BOX 13819 MILWAUKEE, WI 53213

Visit Hal Leonard Online at
www.halleonard.com

0516

YOU CAN'T BEAT OUR DRUM BOOKS!

Learn to Play the Drumset – Book 1
by Peter Magadini
This unique method starts students out on the entire drumset and teaches them the basics in the shortest amount of time. Book 1 covers basic 4- and 5-piece set-ups, grips and sticks, reading and improvisation, coordination of hands and feet, and features a variety of contemporary and basic rhythm patterns with exercise breakdowns for each.
06620030 Book/CD Pack.. $14.99

Creative Timekeeping For The Contemporary Jazz Drummer
by Rick Mattingly
Combining a variety of jazz ride cymbal patterns with coordination and reading exercises, *Creative Timekeeping* develops true independence: the ability to play any rhythm on the ride cymbal while playing any rhythm on the snare and bass drums. It provides a variety of jazz ride cymbal patterns as well as coordination and reading exercises that can be played along with them. Five chapters: Ride Cymbal Patterns; Coordination Patterns and Reading; Combination Patterns and Reading; Applications; and Cymbal Reading.
06621764 .... $8.95

The Drumset Musician
by Rod Morgenstein and Rick Mattingly
Containing hundreds of practical, usable beats and fills, The Drumset Musician teaches you how to apply a variety of patterns and grooves to the actual performance of songs. The accompanying CD includes demos as well as 14 play-along tracks covering a wide range of rock, blues and pop styles, with detailed instructions on how to create exciting, solid drum parts.
06620011 Book/CD Pack.. $19.99

Drum Aerobics
by Andy Ziker
A 52-week, one-exercise-per-day workout program for developing, improving, and maintaining drum technique. Players of all levels – beginners to advanced – will increase their speed, coordination, dexterity and accuracy. The online audio contains all 365 workout licks, plus play-along grooves in styles including rock, blues, jazz, heavy metal, reggae, funk, calypso, bossa nova, march, mambo, New Orleans 2nd Line, and lots more!
06620137 Book/Online Audio $19.99

40 Intermediate Snare Drum Solos
For Concert Performance
by Ben Hans
This book provides the advancing percussionist with interesting solo material in all musical styles. It is designed as a lesson supplement, or as performance material for recitals and solo competitions. Includes: 40 intermediate snare drum solos presented in easy-to-read notation; a music glossary; Percussive Arts Society rudiment chart; suggested sticking, dynamics and articulation markings; and much more!
06620067 .... $7.99

Joe Porcaro's Drumset Method – Groovin' with Rudiments
Patterns Applied to Rock, Jazz & Latin Drumset
by Joe Porcaro
Master teacher Joe Porcaro presents rudiments at the drumset in this sensational new edition of *Groovin' with Rudiments*. This book is chock full of exciting drum grooves, sticking patterns, fills, polyrhythmic adaptations, odd meters, and fantastic solo ideas in jazz, rock, and Latin feels. The enclosed CD features 99 audio clip examples in many styles to round out this true collection of superb drumming material for every serious drumset performer.
06620129 Book/CD Pack.. $24.99

Show Drumming
The Essential Guide to Playing Drumset for Live Shows and Musicals
by Ed Shaughnessy and Clem DeRosa
Who better to teach you than "America's Premier Showdrummer" himself, Mr. Ed Shaughnessy! Features: a step-by-step walk-through of a simulated show; CD with music, comments & tips from Ed; notated examples; practical tips; advice on instruments; a special accessories section with photos; and more!
06620080 Book/CD Pack.. $16.95

Instant Guide to Drum Grooves
The Essential Reference for the Working Drummer
by Maria Martinez
Become a more versatile drumset player! From traditional Dixieland to cutting-edge hip-hop, Instant Guide to Drum Grooves is a handy source featuring 100 patterns that will prepare working drummers for the stylistic variety of modern gigs. The book includes essential beats and grooves in such styles as: jazz, shuffle, country, rock, funk, New Orleans, reggae, calypso, Brazilian and Latin.
06620056 Book/CD Pack.. $9.95

The Complete Drumset Rudiments
by Peter Magadini
Use your imagination to incorporate these rudimental etudes into new patterns that you can apply to the drumset or tom toms as you develop your hand technique with the Snare Drum Rudiments, your hand and foot technique with the Drumset Rudiments and your polyrhythmic technique with the Polyrhythm Rudiments. Adopt them all into your own creative expressions based on ideas you come up with while practicing.
06620016 Book/CD Pack.. $14.95

Drum Tuning
The Ultimate Guide
by Scott Schroedl
This book/CD pack is designed for drummers of all styles and levels. It contains step-by-step instruction along with over 35 professional photos that allow you to see the tools and tuning techniques up close. Covers: preparation; drumhead basics; drum construction and head properties; tom-toms; snare drum; bassdrum; the drum set as one instrument; drum sounds and tuning over the years; when to change heads; and more.
06620060 Book/CD Pack.. $14.95

0816